# Human Body

book-studio

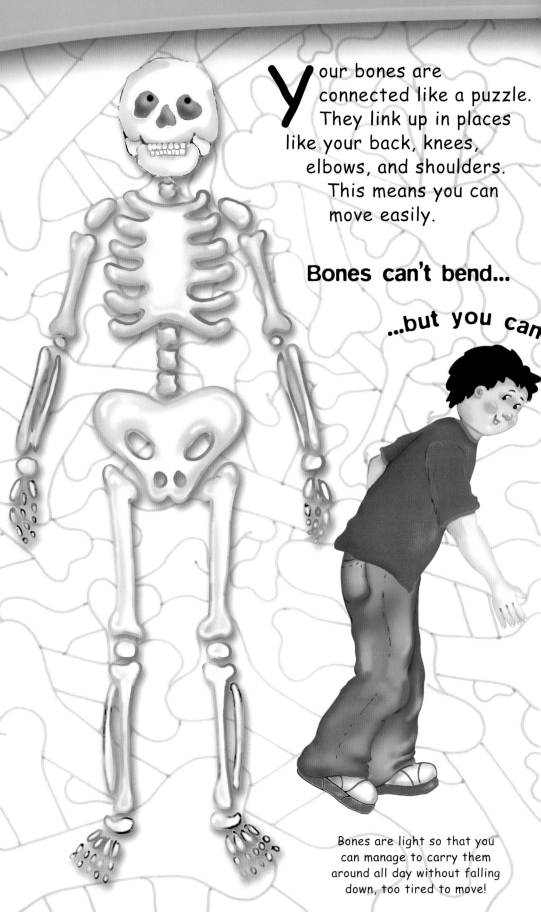

**Y**our bones are connected like a puzzle. They link up in places like your back, knees, elbows, and shoulders. This means you can move easily.

**Bones can't bend...**

**...but you can**

Bones are light so that you can manage to carry them around all day without falling down, too tired to move!

Your bones cannot move on their own. Your muscles move your bones when your brain tells them to.

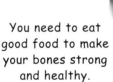

You need to eat good food to make your bones strong and healthy.

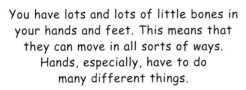

You have lots and lots of little bones in your hands and feet. This means that they can move in all sorts of ways. Hands, especially, have to do many different things.

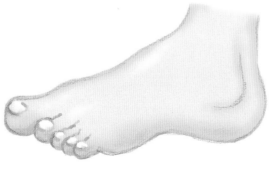

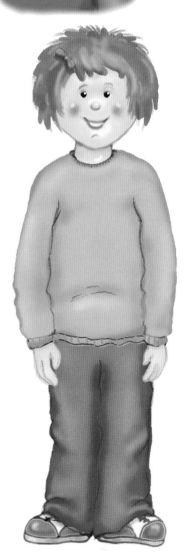

When you sleep, the bones in your back have a chance to stretch out a little. You wake up nearly half an inch (1cm) taller in the morning than when you went to bed!

# Looking inside you

## Your brain is the boss!

Your brain helps you understand what is going on around you—and then tells the rest of your body what to do.

If you pick up something hot, your sense of touch sends a message to the brain which tells your hand to let go—quickly!

## Pumping heart

Your heart is a pump that beats all the time—all your life. It works very hard to pump the blood around your body through 62,000 miles (100,000 km) of blood vessels. That keeps everything working properly.

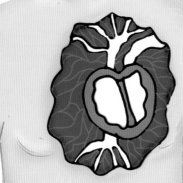

When you run, you can feel your heart beat faster.

# Inside your chest are your lungs

**WHOO OSH!**

Your lungs look like two big sponges and they fill with air when you breathe. To keep working, your body needs air and food—just like a car needs fuel.

**Fuel**

Food goes from your mouth, down into your stomach and then on through the wriggly, squiggly intestines. In a grown-up, food will travel almost 33 feet (10 m).

When your body has taken all the useful stuff it needs, you get rid of the left-over waste by going to the bathroom.

# Muscles

**S**ometimes you use muscles to pull funny faces. Muscles help you to blink, sniff, smile, and frown.

Exercise keeps your muscles strong—and working well.

If you sit around watching television all day long, your muscles will get weak and flabby.

Most muscles help your body to move—when and how you want. You're the boss. When you want to kick that ball your muscles do what you (and your brain) tell them to do.

# Your five senses

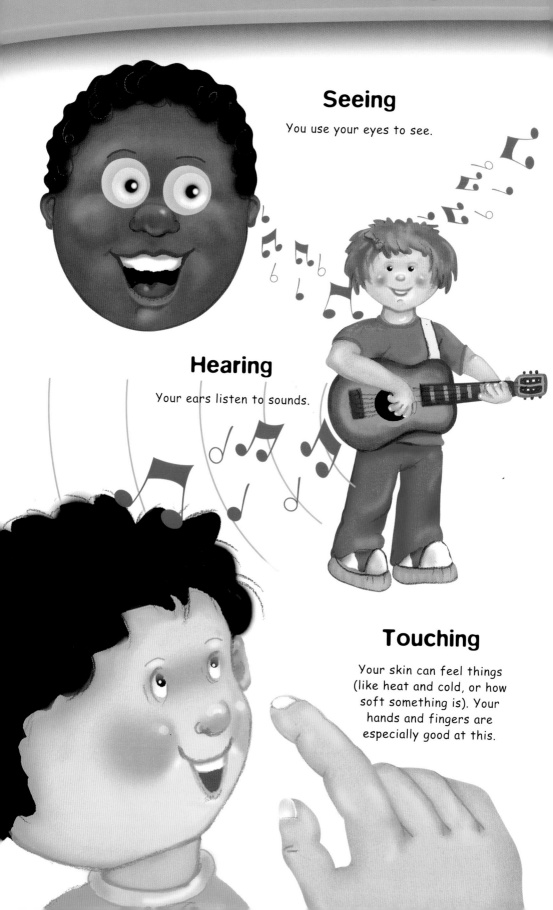

### Seeing
You use your eyes to see.

### Hearing
Your ears listen to sounds.

### Touching
Your skin can feel things (like heat and cold, or how soft something is). Your hands and fingers are especially good at this.

## Smelling

You smell things through your nose. This helps you to enjoy good things like chocolate.

Smell will also warn you of nasty or dangerous things, like bad eggs—or the toast burning! You can pick out up to 4,000 different smells.

## Tasting

Taste buds in your tongue help you decide if something is good or bad to eat.

Your tongue has 10,000 taste buds and can sort out about 500 different tastes.

# Did you know?

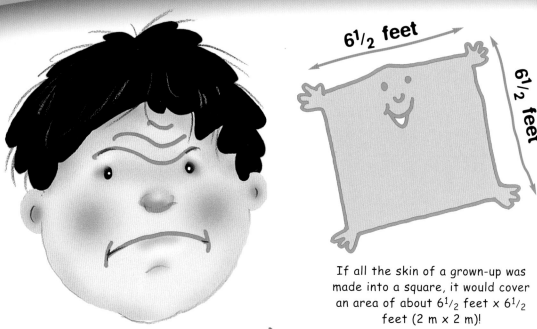

6¹/₂ feet

6¹/₂ feet

If all the skin of a grown-up was made into a square, it would cover an area of about 6¹/₂ feet x 6¹/₂ feet (2 m x 2 m)!

If you frown 2,000 times, it will make a wrinkle!

As you get older your eyes never grow any bigger, but your nose and ears never stop growing!

Your thigh bone is stronger than **concrete!**

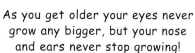

Nerve impulses carry signals to and from your brain at up to 170 miles per hour! (274 km/h).

A lot of your body is made up of water (about 80%). It's not all in one place, it's spread out all around you.

NERVE IMPULSE

You can't sneeze with your eyes open. . .

. . . and when you do sneeze it comes out of your mouth at over 100 miles per hour! (160 km/h)!

# Inside your body ...

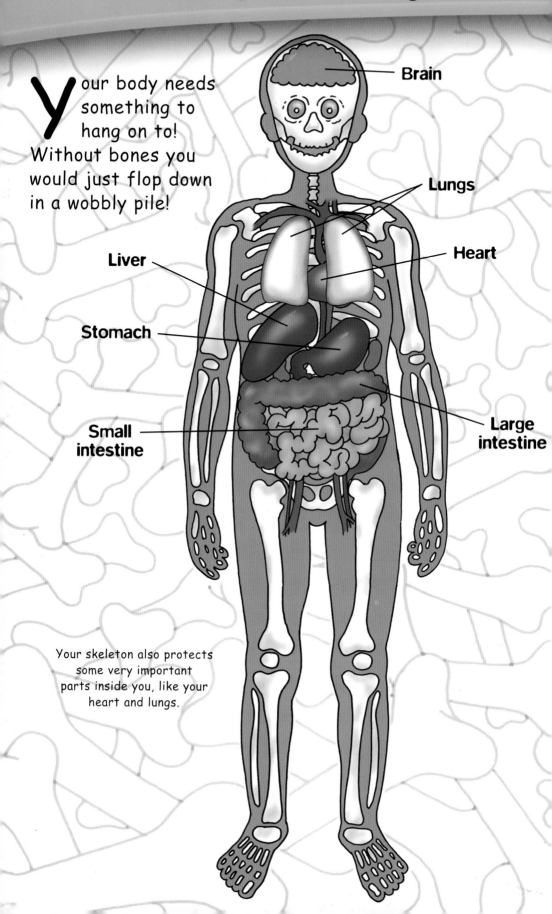

**Y**our body needs something to hang on to! Without bones you would just flop down in a wobbly pile!

Brain

Lungs

Heart

Liver

Stomach

Small intestine

Large intestine

Your skeleton also protects some very important parts inside you, like your heart and lungs.